ML
410   Holst, Imogen
B996   Byrd.
H6

DATE DUE			

Byrd

THE GREAT COMPOSERS

BYRD

IMOGEN HOLST

PRAEGER PUBLISHERS

New York · Washington

BOOKS THAT MATTER

Published in the United States of America in 1972 by
Praeger Publishers, Inc., 111 Fourth Avenue, New York,
N.Y. 10003

Library of Congress Catalog Card Number: 75–188019

Printed in Great Britain

Contents

ACKNOWLEDGEMENTS   *page* 13

NOTES ON THE MUSIC EXAMPLES   15

EXPLANATION OF SOME OF THE
    MUSICAL TERMS   16

I   'Bred up to Music under Tallis'   17

II Organist and Choirmaster of Lincoln
    Cathedral   21

III Gentleman of the Chapel Royal   25

IV Patrons and Pupils   30

V Songs of Sundry Natures   37

VI Viols and Virginals   42

VII Music for the Catholic Church   53

VIII 'This our Golden Age'   59

IX The Last Years at Stondon Massey   63

X Byrd's Music Today   69

SUGGESTIONS FOR FURTHER READING   73

SHORT SUMMARY OF BYRD'S WORKS   74

INDEX   77

Illustrations

Thomas Tallis and William Byrd, from engravings by G. Vandergucht,
1729   *facing page* 16

'Gentlemen of the Chappell', *c.* 1603   17

Angel musicians in a fourteenth-century choir stall at Lincoln
Cathedral   17

The pipe-and-tabor player in the Angel Choir at Lincoln Cathedral:
thirteenth century   32

Detail from a painting of the Thames at Richmond, by David
Vinckeboons (1578–1629)   32

Queen Elizabeth I, soon after her accession, by a contemporary
painter   33

Sir Christopher Hatton, by a contemporary painter   33

Dr. John Bull: a portrait of 1589   48

Sir John Petre: a portrait of 1590   48

The title-page of 'Parthenia', 1612   49

Lord Howard of Effingham, by Daniel Mytens (*c.* 1590–1642)   64

A boy singer and viol players, from a contemporary picture of the
life of Sir Henry Unton (*c.* 1557–96)   65

Ingatestone Hall in Essex   65

LINE ILLUSTRATIONS

Moorfields in 1559   *page* 26

Greenwich Palace in 1543, by A. van den Wyngaerde   28

Decoration used by sixteenth-century English printers   29

Dedication from *A Plain and Easy Introduction to Practical Music* by Thomas Morley, 1597   32

Ornament from a sixteenth-century book   41

A page from 'My Lady Nevell's Book', 1591   44

The beginning of *O Mistress mine*, from Tregian's manuscript, *c.* 1609   45

The Tower of London in 1543, by Wyngaerde   54

A page from Sir John Petre's part-book, *c.* 1580   65

The treble part of 'See those sweet eyes', from *Songs of Sundry Natures*, 1589   70

Music Examples

(The examples are all by Byrd)

Verse from Psalm 55   *page* 19

Canon: *Non nobis, Domine*   20

Canon: *Hey ho! to the greenwood*   33

Canon for four instruments   34

The beginning of a madrigal: *The Nightingale*   38

Prelude   43

Sellenger's Round   46

O Mistress mine   47

Calino Casturame   48

John, come kiss me now   48

Will you walk the woods so wild   49

Walsingham   49

Wolsey's Wild   50

Rowland   52

Kyrie from the *Mass for three voices*   56

Canon: *Pietas omnium virtutum*   57

Amen   58

Deo gratias   66

Acknowledgements

I wish to express my thanks to the following, who have kindly allowed me to reproduce copyright material: to the Trustees of the British Museum for the portraits of Tallis and Byrd, the title-page of *Parthenia* and the line illustrations on pages 32 and 70; to the National Portrait Gallery for the portraits of Queen Elizabeth I, Sir Christopher Hatton, and the detail from the Sir Henry Unton painting; to the Trustees of the London Museum for the illustrations on pages 26, 28 and 54; to the National Maritime Museum, Greenwich Hospital Collection, for the Mytens portrait of Byrd's friend and patron Lord Howard of Effingham; to the Friends of Lincoln Cathedral for their generosity in lending me blocks for two photographs, to the Librarian of Lincoln Cathedral and the Diocesan Archivist for allowing me access to the Muniments Room, and to H. Watkins Shaw for permission to quote from his translation of the Latin entries about Byrd in the Chapter Acts; to the Faculty of Music, Oxford, for the portrait of Dr. John Bull; to the Marquess of Abergavenny for the page from 'My Lady Nevell's Book' and for the privilege of studying the original manuscript in his home; to the Syndics of the Fitzwilliam Museum, Cambridge, for illustrations on pages 32 and 45 and for Ex. 7–14; to the Royal Musical Association for Ex. 6, attributed to Byrd, from *Musica Britannica*, vol. XX, edited by Gerald Hendrie (all other music examples are from sixteenth- and early seventeenth-century editions); to Lord Petre and the Essex Record Office for the portrait of Sir John Petre, the page from his part-book, and the view of Ingatestone Hall; also to the Essex Record Office for quotations from 'English History from Essex Sources', and detailed information from manuscript volumes concerning Stondon Massey; to the Oxford University Press for quotations from *William Byrd* by E. H. Fellowes; to J. G. O'Leary for quotations from his article in 'Essex Recusant', vol. 7, no. 1; to Longman Group Ltd., for information from Philip Caraman's *Henry Garnet* and *The Other Face*; to the BBC Transcription Service for quotations from my article on 'Music in Shakespeare's England'; and to Mr. Stephen Tillyard and Chatto and Windus Ltd., for the paragraph on page 61 from E. M. W. Tillyard's *The Elizabethan World Picture*.

I am also grateful to F. G. Emmison for the advice he gave me when he was County Archivist for Essex; to Arthur Harrison for his help with translating Byrd's Latin dedications; and to Phillis Cunnington for encouraging me to ask for the portrait of Byrd to be reversed so that it is shown the other way round from the engraved copy in the British Museum.

Notes on the Music Examples

In the canon, *Hey ho! to the greenwood* (Ex. 3) the asterisks show where each voice is to enter, and the pause in brackets where each voice is to end. The repeat can be made as many times as one likes: three times through would be a suitable number. If it is sung by mixed voices, the men should come in at the third entry. In Ex. 16 the men's voices should come in on the second entry, as this makes a more satisfactory ending. All canons should have a good deal of variety between loud and soft singing: for instance, the first time through could be *mf*, the second time *p* and the last time *f*. The canon for instruments (Ex. 4) is from Morley's *A Plain and Easy Introduction to Practical Music*: it might have been meant for viols but here it is transcribed for recorders. If the quick tunes from the 'Fitzwilliam Virginal Book' (Ex. 7–14) are too difficult for one player they can be tried out by two players as a duet: it is for this reason that no fingering has been given. In Ex. 5 it is tantalizing to have to stop half-way through, but the example would have taken up too many pages in the book: the complete madrigal, from *Songs of Sundry Natures*, is published by Stainer and Bell, edited by E. H. Fellowes. The 'Amen' (Ex. 17) is from the 'Magnificat' in Byrd's *Second Service*.

A SHORT EXPLANATION OF SOME OF THE
MUSICAL TERMS USED IN THIS BOOK

page 18   polyphonic: 'many-sounding', or 'many-voiced'

18   motet: a sacred song or anthem with Latin words

19   plainsong, or plainchant: a freely flowing medieval Latin chant, as sung in the Roman Catholic church

19   round or canon: a tune that is sung by several voices, entering one after another; in a round the second voice enters when the first voice has reached the end of a sentence; in a canon the second voice enters much sooner

37   madrigal: a secular polyphonic part-song in the 'mother-tongue'

42   Fantasia: an instrumental piece with many entries in imitation

42   antiphon: a short religious text sung to plainsong

43   Pavan (or Pavane): a slow dignified dance

43   Galliard: a quick gay dance in triple time

69–70   semibreve: whole note, minim: half note, crotchet: quarter note, quaver: eighth note

Above, Thomas Tallis and, *below*, William Byrd

Above, 'Gentlemen of the Chapell', c. 1603; below, angel musicians in a fourteenth-century choir stall at Lincoln Cathedral

I

'Bred up to music under Tallis'

When William Byrd died at the age of eighty he was known as 'a famous man of skill', the greatest among the many great English composers of his time. The date of his death was recorded in a black leather-bound register of musicians employed by James I: 'Wm. Byrd, a Father of Music, died the 4th of July, 1623.'

There is no record of the date of his birth. We know that it was some time in 1543, because in his will, which he wrote during the last winter of his life, he happened to mention that he was in his eightieth year. But we know nothing about his birthplace nor his parents. Historians have searched for information, but no facts are known about his life until he was twenty. If we try to imagine how he spent his first nineteen years we can only rely on the few hints that have survived from the sixteenth century: a couple of lines in a Latin poem by a rich amateur musician; a sentence from the diary of a priest in hiding; or a few words scribbled in the margin of a manuscript part-book.

His father may have been Thomas Byrd, one of the singers who earned sevenpence a day in the Chapel Royal at the end of Henry VIII's reign. The musicians in the King's employment were chosen from among the best in the whole country, and during the 1550s these Gentlemen of the Chapel Royal would often have been in and out of Thomas Byrd's house, for he was 'Clerk of the Cheque', which meant that he was responsible for entering all details in the account book whenever a singer was away from work or a new member was appointed to the choir. Foreign musicians on a visit to England might also have found their way to the Byrds' house. There is a legend that the eleven-year-old William made friends with the Flemish composer Philippe de Monte, who was one of the distinguished musicians Philip II of Spain brought with him to England to celebrate his marriage with Queen Mary. Thirty years later, Byrd and de Monte were sending each other their newest compositions, half-way across Europe, with warm-hearted greetings.

William had probably begun composing before he was eleven, for we are told he was 'bred up to music under Tallis', who was 'a great master, and worthy of all honour'. Thomas Tallis's own teachers had been writing at the end of the fifteenth century, when music was still in the period that is sometimes described as 'late medieval'. There was nothing primitive about it. English cathedral music in 1500 could be as magnificently elaborate as the fan-vaulting of the high roofs under which it was sung. Today, when we look up at the ceiling of King's College Chapel in Cambridge or of St. George's Chapel at Windsor, we can see how the delicate tracery spreads outwards from each strong centre of support. And when we listen to one of the polyphonic, 'many-voiced' motets of Tallis's predecessors we can hear the delicate, interweaving patterns of sound spreading outwards from the strong, supporting framework of their harmony.

Tallis went further than his teachers in exploring the possibilities of these interweaving patterns. His most famous motet, *Spem in alium*, is for as many as forty solo voices. This is music that needs the resonance of a large church or cathedral: when the eight distantly-placed five-part choirs combine to build up the climax of their prayer to 'the Creator of heaven and earth', the sound is overwhelming.

While he was writing this motet, Tallis may have remembered the echoes in those wide aisles at Waltham Abbey in Essex, where he had been employed during the late 1530s. The few years that he spent there had been over-shadowed by anxiety about the future. Henry VIII was seizing hundreds of monasteries throughout England, and in 1539 a statute was passed which gave him the right to confiscate all the remaining monastic houses. The Augustinian Abbey of the Holy Cross at Waltham was the very last to be closed down, and in 1540 Tallis was having to look for work elsewhere.

The dissolution of the monasteries put an end to many traditions of music-making and led to the disappearance of many libraries of books and music. An eye-witness has said that the rich people who bought the monasteries seized the library books for themselves, 'some to scour their candlesticks, and some to rub their boots. Some they sold to the grocers and soap-sellers, and some they sent oversea to the bookbinders, not in small numbers but at times whole shipsful, to the wondering of the foreign nations.'

Fortunately one of the Waltham Abbey music books has survived. It is called 'Liber Sanctae Crucis de Waltham', and it is safely housed in the British Museum in London. The lively details of each illuminated initial are still as brilliantly coloured as when the book was written. There are examples of the use of the clefs, and practical hints on counterpoint by the fifteenth-century composer Leonel Power, who liked finding out different ways to help anyone who wished to sing 'mannerly and musically'. Tallis wrote his name on the last page of the book, and he must have taught some of the lessons in it to his young pupil William Byrd, because years later, when Byrd himself was a teacher, he quoted from it to his own pupils.

There were many other things that Tallis could teach him. He learnt some of the plainsong hymns the monks had chanted, and which he afterwards used in his own motets. He learnt to write rounds and canons, such as *Non nobis, Domine*, and to search for the 'true notes' of those simple 'tuneable tunes' that could be enjoyed by singers and players and listeners; tunes such as the Tallis hymn that is still sung to the words 'Praise God from whom all blessings flow'.

We are told that Byrd also learnt 'to play the organ and many other instruments'. He must have been a particularly brilliant organ pupil because when he was only just twenty he was offered the important post of organist at the cathedral in Lincoln, which was then one of the chief cities of England.

Ex. 1   Verse from Psalm 55

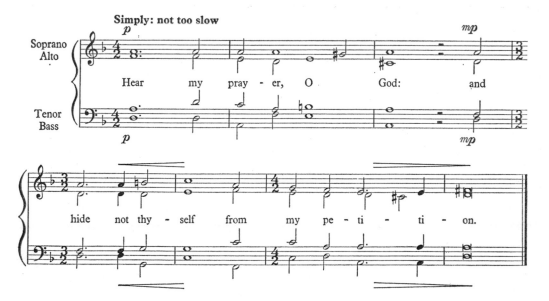

Ex. 2 Canon: *Non nobis, Domine*

II

Organist and Choirmaster of Lincoln Cathedral

In the cathedral account books at Lincoln there is an entry, dated April 24th, 1563, which says: 'Know ye that we, the dean and chapter, have given to William Byrd the post of master of the chorister boys, with all wages belonging to the said post, namely six pounds thirteen shillings and fourpence of legal English money. We have also granted to the same William Byrd the post of player at the organs . . . with all wages pertaining to which post, namely six pounds thirteen shillings and fourpence.'

An income of just over thirteen pounds may not seem much to live on even when we realize the immense difference in the value of money in 1563. Byrd's salary, however, was larger than most other cathedral organists were earning, for Lincoln was such an important city.

The huge west front of the cathedral still looks much the same as it did when Byrd walked across the close every morning on his way to work. The carved stone figures on either side of the door, representing the banishment from the Garden of Eden and the building of Noah's Ark, were already more than four hundred years old when he first stood there and looked up at them. Inside the cathedral, high up between the spandrells of the chancel arches, the thirteenth-century stone angels still hold their musical instruments. They are playing harps and trumpets, which is only to be expected in a building intended for the singing of psalms. But they are also playing the pipe and tabor, which were never intended for anything but dance music. Twentieth-century sightseers are sometimes astonished to find such cheerful instruments in such pious hands, but that is because they are thinking of 'sacred' and 'secular' as labels attached to two different kinds of art. Byrd would have taken the pipe and tabor for granted. And he would have felt no surprise at seeing the love-story of Tristan and Isolde carved in oak under one of the fourteenth-century choir-stalls where his singers sat each Sunday.

On week-days he taught in the choir school, 'well and diligently instructing the choristers'. The cathedral had had a good reputation for music-making. Byrd's predecessor, the 'skilled and faithful' Thomas Appleby, was organist there for more than twenty years, but he had been unable to protest when the number of his vicars-choral had shrunk from twenty-five to twelve. This recent economy was one of the results of the Reformation.

During the twenty years of Byrd's life there had been as many as four monarchs ruling over England, and each had introduced changes in the established religion. Henry VIII had declared that his subjects were 'devout catholics', but that 'the English Church' was 'sufficient of itself'. By the time Byrd was six years old, Edward VI's 'Book of Common Prayer' was in use, 'to be said or sung' throughout England, and a law was passed, stating that 'henceforth choristers shall sing no anthems of our lady or other saints, but only of our Lord, and then not in Latin.'. The Archbishop of Canterbury, Thomas Cranmer, was busy uprooting the 'relics of popery', while Ridley, the Bishop of London, took only a week to get rid of the altars in all the churches of his diocese. There were people in nearly every parish in England who missed the old ritual with its processions by candlelight and its clouds of incense rising up to the brightly-coloured images of the saints. Those who felt most strongly about it had the courage to march in protest against the government: they were tried as rebels and hanged for treason. In 1553, when Byrd was about ten years old, the Catholic Queen Mary came to the throne and the new victims of change were the Protestant reformers of the previous reign. Three hundred of these martyrs were burned at the stake, including Ridley and Cranmer. England was once more a Catholic country, and choristers were again singing plainchant and Latin anthems. Five years later Queen Elizabeth I began her long reign, and within a very few months 'no Mass was said any more' by order of Parliament. Church-wardens of each parish were being told 'to wash out of the walls all paintings that seemed to be Romish'; and the Abbot of Westminster was complaining in the House of Lords that all things were changed and 'turned upside down'.

English church-going families must have lived in a state of bewilderment from one reign to the next. Some of their practical difficulties are recorded in their parish registers:

1550   For taking down the altars and carrying away the rubbish, 3s.
       Other expenses at the removing thereof, 6d.
1554   Making of the altar, 2s. 4d.

For the three images painting, 6s. 8d.

1559   For pulling down the altar, 2d.

For blotting out the images, 4d.

The reformers of 1559 would have liked to have destroyed all the saints in the stained-glass windows. But here they had to move cautiously, for glass was expensive and churches were cold. So the windows were 'not altogether abolished in most places at once, but by little and little suffered to decay'. It was a typically English compromise.

Queen Elizabeth's rules about church services stated that there should be 'a modest and distinct song that may be as plainly understanded as if it were read without singing'. This had been Archbishop Cranmer's advice, when he said that English church music should not be 'full of notes, but, as near as may be, for every syllable a note'. These rules had only recently been proclaimed when Byrd arrived at Lincoln, but already a beginning had been made in the new style. His teacher, Tallis, had written a 'Short Service' for Edward VI. In 1560 a Londoner called John Day had published 'Certain notes set forth in four parts, to be sung at the morning and evening prayer, very necessary for the church'. Two years later the same publisher produced 'The whole book of Psalms, collected into English metre, with apt notes to sing them withal'. This, the first English hymn-book, was used by 'all the congregation, men, women and boys singing to-gether': it contained the newly-written tune 'All people that on earth do dwell'.

Byrd's own inclination was for polyphonic motets 'full of notes', with long, flowing passages to a single Latin syllable. But he was a practical com-poser who knew that his job was to provide what was wanted. His simple English settings are beautifully balanced phrases; and, unlike some of the nineteenth-century responses, his harmonies always manage to suit the words of each new verse.

His duties at Lincoln included 'diligently exercising the post of player at the organs'. He must have improvised a good deal of the time, and not much has survived to suggest what he may have played while the clergy were processing into the chancel. But from later collections of his key-board music we know that he enjoyed playing Variations on the Hexa-chord (six stepwise notes of a scale with the semitone in the middle), with moods changing from slow and solemn to brilliant and sprightly.

The cathedral authorities had asked Byrd to stay at Lincoln 'until the end of his natural life', if he were 'willing so long to occupy the post'. He stayed for ten years. The few facts that are known about his life there have had to be pieced together from entries in the Lincoln archives. During his first year 'the scarcity of all kinds of grain and victuals' had been so appalling that the mayor and justices had not known what to do about it. In the following summer the city shopkeepers had revived the tradition of the medieval guild plays, and had given an open-air performance, but we are not told whether anyone had thought of asking the new young organist to help with the music.

The account books in the cathedral show entries for providing 'paper and ink for William Byrd', who was industriously teaching his choristers. There was one occasion when the dean and chapter objected to his over-elaborate organ-playing before the chanting of the Te Deum and the Magnificat. (This is the usual sort of complaint that church authorities make when they find to their embarrassment that they employing a genius.) On the whole, however, they were well-disposed towards him, and they allowed him to live rent-free in a house in the cathedral close.

The parish registers of the church of St. Margaret's-in-the-Close prove that he was married there to Juliana Birley on September 14th, 1568, and that his eldest son Christopher was baptized there on November 18th, 1569.

On the day after this christening ceremony there was a meeting of the cathedral chapter to which Byrd, for some unknown reason, was summoned in disgrace. Historians have suggested that he may have been making too many visits to London, for it was only three months later that he was elected a Gentleman of the Chapel Royal. Or it may be that some of the clergy accused him of preferring what they called 'the superstitious Latin service', knowing that he was still a Catholic. Whatever the 'certain matters of objection' may have been, the authorities withdrew their threat to stop his salary, and he stayed for another three years, 'adorning the cathedral by his skill'. Then, at the end of 1572, he took his family to London, having been invited to share with Tallis the post of organist at the Chapel Royal.

III

Gentleman of the Chapel Royal

The word 'chapel' suggests a building, but in the name 'Chapel Royal' it is used in its medieval sense, to describe a group of musicians employed by a king or queen. These singers and players travelled from place to place with their instruments and their part-books, providing the music for church services in the chapel of whichever royal palace the sovereign happened to be staying in at the time. During Byrd's life the most important of the royal residences was Whitehall Palace, a vast, rambling building with hundreds of rooms, and with courtyards and gardens spreading across twenty acres. All that is left of the Tudor palace that Byrd knew is Henry VIII's wine-cellar near the Banqueting House in Whitehall. Among the other royal palaces, Hampton Court has not altered much since his time, and at Windsor there is still the same St. George's chapel where his friends from the Chapel Royal sometimes sang with the resident choir; but the palace at Greenwich is no longer the same building in which he and Tallis worked together during the fifteen-seventies. Queen Elizabeth's favourite palace, Nonesuch, has completely disappeared, and only a few fragments are left of Richmond Palace where she died. In Richmond, however, we can see glimpses of the countryside that Byrd must have known so well: the towing-path is still muddy and uneven to walk on, and across the river one can see and hear the sheep in the lower meadow at Syon House.

The London of four hundred years ago was so much smaller than today's London that we need to look at an old map to realize how our built-up areas were then open country. An illustrated plan of the city, drawn when Byrd was still a child, shows the Moor Field just beyond Bishopsgate with washer-women spreading out their laundry on the grass, while cattle graze in a meadow near the Finsbury windmills. By the end of the sixteenth century London's population had grown to nearly two hundred thousand, and we are told that 'ships from France, the Netherlands, Sweden, Denmark and other kingdoms' were coming 'almost up to the city'. Londoners were com-

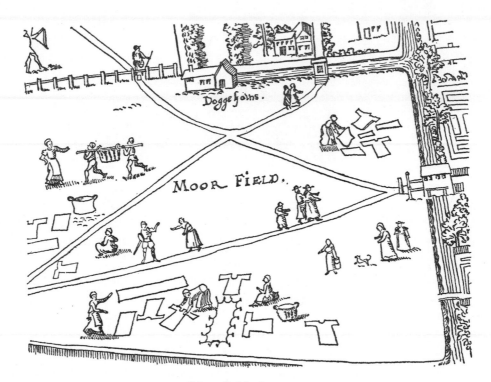

Moorfields in 1559

plaining about overcrowding, saying: 'one can scarcely pass along the streets on account of the throng'. Many of these sixteenth-century complaints sound familiar: if it were not for their idiom they might almost have been written for the correspondence columns of a London newspaper in the nineteen-seventies. There were complaints about modern architecture: 'houses so full of glass that one cannot tell where to be out of the sun'. There were complaints about 'the prices of things becoming excessive', and about smoking at meals: 'puffing of the tobacco one to another when very often men that abhor it are at their repast'. Football was condemned as 'rather a kind of fight than a recreation'. Young men were blamed for 'wearing their hair so long' that it made them look 'like a water-spaniel'; while the young women were 'not content with their own hair', but bought 'other hair of horses or strange beasts, dyeing it of what colour they list'. And the newest 1577 fashion in clothes made it difficult to discern 'whether they were men or women'.

There were also complaints about the noise of the traffic 'thundering as if the world ran upon wheels'. But their wheels were very different from ours, for they belonged to the leisurely carts and the cumbersome coaches that were cluttering the streets.

Byrd could not afford a coach, so he rode to work on horseback. The journeys were long and tiring, for he had chosen to make his home at Harlington in Middlesex. There is a tradition that his house was 'in the middle of the village, near the pond'. (The pond is still where it was, but the roaring aeroplanes over Heathrow make it difficult to imagine a composer writing his music there.)

He probably decided to settle in Harlington because it was easier for Catholic families to keep to their own ways when they lived outside London. He was already known as a 'recusant' because he was opposed to the established religion, and during the fifteen-seventies his wife's name was included in a list of those who were fined for refusing to attend the Sunday services at Harlington parish church.

In spite of being a recusant, Byrd wrote settings of the English Matins and Evensong that are as beautiful as any of his other music. The Queen had encouraged the writing of anthems, saying: 'for the comforting of such as delight in music, it may be permitted that in the beginning or the end of common prayers, there may be sung an hymn or such-like song . . . in the best sort of melody and music that may be devised'. It was certainly the best sort of music that was sung in the Chapel Royal. A scrap of conversation heard on a Sunday morning in 1573 has survived:

'Harken, I do hear a sweet music!'
'See whether we may get to the choir, and we shall hear the fairest voices of all the cathedral churches in England.'
'I believe you: who should have them if the Londoners had them not?'
'I think that the Queen's singing men are there.'
'That may be: for, to tell the truth, I never heard better singing.'

In the Chapel Royal they were allowed to sing motets in Latin; a special privilege that was shared with the college chapels at Oxford and Cambridge, 'for the further encouraging of learning in the Latin tongue'. Many church-goers objected to this, condemning it as 'a cloaked papistry or mingle-mangle'. A zealous parson said: 'the Queen's Chapel, which should be a spectacle of Christian reformation, is rather a pattern of all superstition.' (It was this parson who, in the month when Byrd arrived, had complained: 'they toss the psalms like tennis-balls!')

There were other church-goers, however, who said that a motet could draw the listener into 'a devout and reverent kind of consideration of him

Greenwich Palace in 1543, by A. van den Wyngaerde

for whose praise it was made'. And it was with these listeners in mind that Byrd and Tallis wrote their 1575 volume of *Cantiones Sacrae*, a collection of Latin motets, of which half were by Tallis and half by Byrd. They had chosen their texts carefully, taking the words from psalms, or from prayers for Holy Week or hymns to the Trinity, and avoiding any mention of the Virgin Mary or the saints. They dedicated the volume to the Queen as a thank-you for the licence to print music which she had just granted them. In this document she had announced:

To all printers and booksellers: Know ye, that we for the especial affection and good will that we have and bear unto the science of music and for the advancement thereof . . . have granted full privilege and licence unto our wellbeloved servants Thomas Tallis and William Byrd, Gentlemen of our Chapel . . . to imprint so many as they will of set songs or songs in parts, either in English, Latin, French, Italian or other tongues

28

that may serve for music either in church or chamber, or otherwise to be either played or sung.

The *Cantiones Sacrae* was the first volume to be printed under the new licence, and it was with high hopes for the future that the two composers wrote their introductory dedication to the Queen, turning to her 'as to a patron'.

Decoration used by sixteenth-century English printers

IV

Patrons and Pupils

The Queen's licence to print music was meant to help Byrd and Tallis, but before long they found they were losing money instead of making a profit. It is not that they were unbusinesslike. Monopolies were a mixed blessing, and even as experienced a man as the Queen's printer of books was soon having to admit that patents were 'of much less value than before, and like to be rather worse than better', and that a privilege could prove 'more dangerous to the patentee than profitable'.

Byrd now had three children to support, and Tallis was over seventy, so they decided to ask the Queen for a lease in reversion on some rented property, which was a usual form of payment in those days. Their petition, addressed 'to the Queen's most excellent Majesty', was endorsed 'at Greenwich, the 27th of June, 1577':

Most humbly beseech your Majesty your poor servants Thomas Tallis and William Byrd, Gentlemen of your highness' Chapel. That whereas the said Thomas Tallis is now very aged and hath served your Majesty and your Royal ancestors these forty years, and had as yet never any manner of preferment (except only one lease which your Majesty's late dear sister Queen Mary gave him, which lease being now the best part of his living is within one year of expiration . . .). And also for that the said William Byrd being called to your highness' service from the cathedral church of Lincoln where he was well settled is now through his great charge of wife and children come into debt and great necessity, by reason that by his daily attendance in your Majesty's service he is letted [that is, prevented] from reaping such commodity by teaching as heretofore he did and still might have done to the great relief of himself and his poor family: And further, your Majesty of your princely goodness intending the benefit of us your said poor servants did give unto us about two years past a licence for the printing of music. So it is, most gracious Sovereign, that the same hath fallen out to our great loss and hindrance to the value of two hundred marks at the least. It might therefore please your Majesty of your most abundant goodness for the better relieving of our poor estates To grant unto us a lease in reversion . . . So shall we most dutifully pray unto almighty God for the prosperous preservation of your Majesty long to Reign over us.

It is good to know that 'it pleased her Majesty' to grant the petitioners their request 'in consideration of their good service done to her highness'.

The Queen had proved to be a helpful patron of music, and people were saying that 'if it were not for the Queen's majesty, singing-men and choristers might go a-begging'. Byrd was grateful to her, but, like other composers of his time, he needed help from more than one patron if he was to succeed in earning an adequate living. In the mid-fifteen-seventies several 'noblemen and councillors' were writing 'gracious letters' on his behalf. He was clever in his choice of patrons, realizing that he would have to rely on their influence at court and their sympathy with Catholic recusants, as well as on their love of music.

Sir Christopher Hatton, to whom Byrd dedicated his first volume of English songs, was Lord Chancellor of England. He was also an amateur actor and playwright, and he had known Byrd in the fifteen-sixties, when they had worked together on a tragedy called *Tancred and Gismunda*.

The Earl of Northumberland was another powerful friend and patron. In 1579, when Byrd was having difficulties over an unjust law-suit, Northumberland wrote a personal letter to the Lord High Treasurer on Byrd's behalf, in which he said: 'I am the more importunate to your lordship for that he is my friend, and chiefly that he is schoolmaster to my daughter in his art. The man is honest, and one whom I know your lordship may commend'.

The 'schoolmaster' in Byrd has been immortalized by his best pupil, Thomas Morley, who wrote a text-book for beginners called *A Plain and Easy Introduction to Practical Music*. It is a long, intricate book, closely packed with technical information, but Morley has a lively way of writing, and there are occasional hints of the never-to-be-forgotten lessons he had once learnt from his great master. He dedicated the book to Byrd, saying: 'these labours of mine [I have published] under your name, both to signify unto the world my thankful mind, and also to notify unto yourself the entire love and unfeigned affection which I bear unto you. Accept (I pray you) of this book, both that you may exercise your deep skill in censuring of what shall be

To the moſt excellent Mu-
ſician Maiſter William Birde
one of the gentlemen of her
Maieſties chappell.

THere be two whoſe benifites to vs can neuer be
requited: God,and our parents, the one for that
he gaue vs a reaſonable ſoule,the other for that of
thē we haue our beeing.To theſe the prince &(as
Cicero tearmeth him)the God of the *Philoſophers*
added our maiſters,as thoſe by whoſe directions
the faculties ofthe reaſonable ſoule be ſtirred vp
to enter into contemplation,& ſearching of more
then earthly things:whereby we obtaine a ſecond
being,more to be wiſhed and much more durable
thē that which any man ſince the worlds creatiō hath receiued of his parents:
cauſing vs liue in the mindes ofthe vertuous,as it were,deified to the poſte-
ritie. The conſideration of this hath moued me to publiſh theſe labors of
mine vnder your name both to ſignifie vnto the world, my thankfull mind:&
alſo to notifie vnto your ſelfe in ſome ſort the entire loue and vnfained affection which I beare vnto you. And ſeeing we liue in thoſe daies wherein enuie
raigneth;and that it is neceſſary for him who ſhall put to light any ſuch thing
as this is,to chooſe ſuch a patron,as both with iudgement may correct it, and
with authority defend him from the raſh cenſures of ſuch as thinke they gaine
great praiſe in condemning others:Accept (I pray you) of this booke, both
that you may exerciſe your deepe skill in cenſuring of what ſhall be amiſſe,as
alſo defend what is in it truely ſpoken,as that which ſomtime proceeded from
your ſelfe. So ſhall your approbation cauſe me thinke the better of it,& your
name ſet in the forefront thereof be ſufficient to abate the furie of many inſul-
ting momiſtes who think nothing true but what they doo themſelues. And as
thoſe verſes were not eſteemed *Homers* which *Ariſtarchus* had not approuod,
ſo wil I not auouch for mine that which by your cenſure ſhalbe condemned.
And ſo I reſt,

In all loue and affection to you moſt addicted,
THOMAS MORLEY.

Dedication from *A Plain and Easy Introduction to Practical Music*
by Thomas Morley, 1597

amiss, as also defend what is in it truly spoken, as that which sometime proceeded from yourself.'

Among the many things in the book which may have proceeded from
Byrd, there is a heartfelt reminder of the fact that when we have gained a

Above, the pipe-and-tabor player in the Angel Choir at Lincoln Cathedral;
below, detail from a painting of the Thames at Richmond, by David Vinckeboons

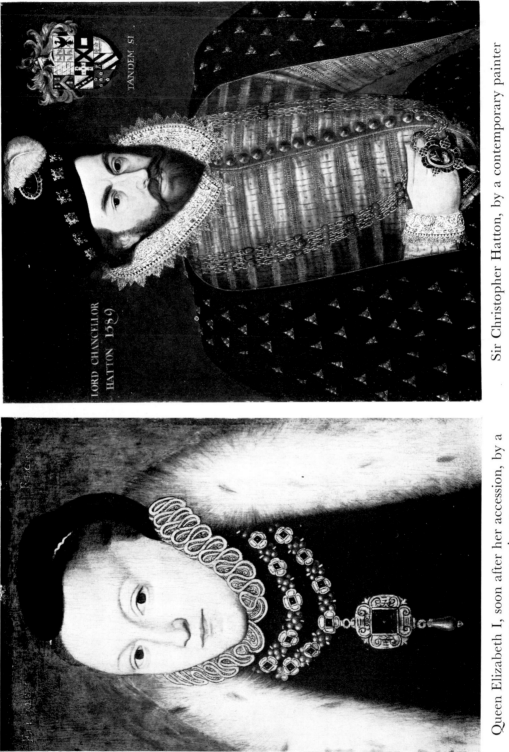

Sir Christopher Hatton, by a contemporary painter

Queen Elizabeth I, soon after her accession, by a contemporary painter

Ex. 3   Canon: *Hey ho! to the greenwood*

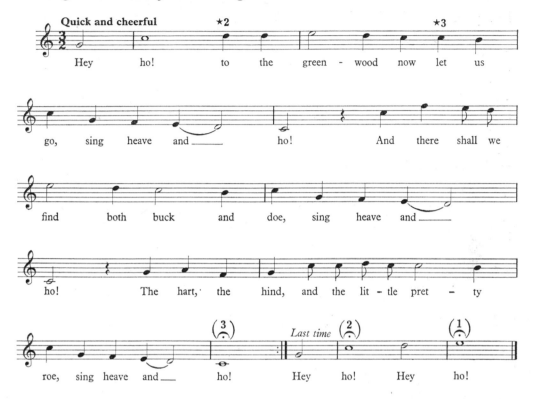

little knowledge 'we straight imagine that we have all, when, God knows, the least part of that which we know *not* is more than all we know'. There are helpful facts for the beginner who is learning harmony: 'you may reckon your chords from your bass upwards or from the tune downward, which you list, for as it is twenty miles from London to Ware, so is it twenty from Ware to London'. And there is an excellent definition of the word 'imitation' in its polyphonic sense: 'we call that Imitation when one part beginneth and the other singeth the same, for some number of notes, which the first did sing'.

Morley's description of 'a great master in music' is one who is so used to writing in canon that 'he may almost at the first sight see what may be done'. He advises the learner to practise writing 'those plain ways of canon, which will, as it were, lead you by the hand to a further knowledge'. And as an example of further knowledge he says: 'I thought good to set down a canon made by Mr Byrd, which for difficulty in the composition is not inferior to any which I have seen, for it is both made by rising and falling and then turned to go the contrary way, note for note.' (See Ex. 4.)

Ex. 4 Canon for four instruments

Flowing

Descant
Recorder
1

Descant
Recorder
2

Descant
Recorder
3

Treble
or
Tenor
Recorder

rall.

The 'Plain and Easy Introduction' is written in the form of a dialogue between Pupil and Master. At one point the harassed Pupil says: 'I have had so many observations that I pray God I may keep them all in mind.' The Master replies: 'The best means to keep them in mind is continually to be practising . . . When you have any friend to sing with you, you may practise together, which will sooner make you perfect than if you should study never so much by yourself.'

The Master warns his Pupil to keep to the most comfortable range of notes for the voices; if he writes too low, the voice will 'seem as a kind of humming', and if the notes are too high, the result will be 'a kind of constrained shrieking'. Morley would certainly have had lessons in writing for voices from his own master, because Byrd cared so much about good singing that he published his own *Reasons briefly set down to persuade everyone to learn to sing*:

FIRST it is a knowledge easily taught and quickly learnt, where there is a good master and an apt scholar.
2. The exercise of singing is delightful to nature and good to preserve the health of man.
3. It doth strengthen all parts of the breast, and doth open the pipes.
4. It is a singular good remedy for a stutting and stammering in the speech.
5. It is the best means to procure a perfect pronunciation and to make a good orator.
6. It is the only way to know where nature hath bestowed the benefit of a good voice: which gift is so rare as there is not one among a thousand that hath it: and in many that excellent gift is lost, because they want art to express nature.
7. There is not any music of instruments whatsoever, comparable to that which is made of the voices of men, where the voices are good and the same well sorted and ordered.
8. The better the voice is, the meeter it is to honour and serve God therewith: and the voice of man is chiefly to be employed to that end.

Omnis spiritus laudet Dominum.

Since singing is so good a thing,
I wish all men would learn to sing.

V

Songs of Sundry Natures

Byrd's 'Reasons' for persuading everyone to sing were published at the beginning of his 1588 *Psalms, Sonnets and Songs*. In his introduction to the 'benign reader' he says:

Here is offered unto thy courteous acceptation, music of sundry sorts, and to content diverse humours. If thou be disposed to pray, here are psalms. If to be merry, here are sonnets. If to lament thy sins, here are songs of sadness and piety. . . . Whatsoever pains I have taken herein, I shall think to be well employed if the same be well accepted, music thereby the better loved and the more exercised. . . . If thou find anything here worthy of liking and commendation, give praise unto God, from whom (as a most pure and plentiful fountain) all good gifts do flow: whose name be glorified for ever.

> The most assured friend to
> all that love or learn music:
> WILLIAM BYRD

The songs, which were 'made into music of five parts', were written 'for the recreation of all such as delight in music'. They were published in separate part-books, and Byrd mentions that he decided to allow them to be printed because he had found so many 'untrue, incorrected copies' in manuscript that he felt the time had come to make 'truly corrected' copies available to his many good friends who had so often asked for them.

This 1588 collection was only the third English song book ever to have been published. Madrigals had at first been thought of as Italian songs, and 'books of that kind were yearly sent out of Italy'. An enthusiastic singer called Nicholas Yonge had the sensible idea of getting these madrigals translated from Italian into English, and on the title-page of his *Musica Transalpina* he mentions, by way of advertisement, that it contains *La Virginella*, 'made by Master Byrd upon two stanzas of Ariosto, and brought to speak English with the rest'.

Ex. 5 The beginning of a madrigal: *The Nightingale*

Songs of Sundry Natures

Byrd had included *La Virginella* in his 1588 *Psalms, Sonnets and Songs,* and the book was such a success that he was able to bring out another, called *Songs of Sundry Natures,* the very next year. He dedicated it to Lord Hunsdon, the Lord Chamberlain, hoping that the songs would delight his lordship after he had been 'forewearied in affairs of great importance'.

There were newly-written English poems for him to set to music in these two books. He chose dancing rhymes and rhythms for those of his singers who wished to be merry, but being by nature 'disposed to gravity' his own preference was for the songs of sadness and piety. Among the laments there is a passionate elegy for the martyred Catholic, Edmund Campion:

> *Why do I use my paper, ink, and pen,*
> *And call my wits to counsel what to say?*
> *Such memories were made for mortal men,*
> *I speak of saints whose names cannot decay.*
> *An angel's trump were fitter for to sound*
> *Their glorious death, if such on earth were found.*

The thought of his fellow-recusants can seldom have been far from his mind: we can recognize it in the metrical psalms he included in these English song-books:

> *In misty clouds of troubles dark,*
> *Which do the just oppress,*
> *The Lord in mercy sends them light*
> *And easeth their distress.*

It is in his choice of verses about quiet contentment that we can perhaps come nearest to a glimpse of his own character:

> *My mind to me a Kingdom is,*
> *Such perfect joy therein I find*
> *That it excells all other bliss,*
> *Which God or Nature hath assigned;*
> *Though much I want that most would have,*
> *Yet still my mind forbids to crave.*

That song, like most of the others in the 1588 collection, was not originally meant to be sung by unaccompanied voices: it was 'made for instruments to express the harmony, and one voice to pronounce the ditty'. In the more elaborate settings his amateur singers and players cannot have found it easy to keep together, and there must have been many occasions when they got out of time and had to stop and begin again. Byrd realized this, and he mentioned in the introduction to *Songs of Sundry Natures* that some of the songs were easy to sing, 'others more hard and difficult, but all, such as any young practitioner in singing, with a little foresight, may easily perform'.

The illustration facing page 65 shows a young boy-treble of the fifteen-nineties singing the ditty while the instruments 'express the harmony'. It is obvious that he has more than a little 'foresight'. He is catching the eye of the leading viol player with that determined yet flexible courtesy which is the essence of true chamber-music in any century.

Ornament from a sixteenth-century book

VI

Viols and Virginals

The viols that Byrd was writing for sounded quite different from a string quartet, for they belonged to a different family of instruments. The viol began life in fifteenth-century Spain as a guitar that was played with a bow: its name was *vihuela de arco*. In the sixteenth century it had six strings, tuned in fourths with a major third in the middle; and it was made in four sizes: treble, alto, tenor and bass.

All viols, even the smallest, are held downwards, instead of being supported under the chin like the violin. And all viols, like their ancestor the guitar, are fretted with bits of gut tied round the finger-board a semitone apart. People sometimes imagine that this is just to help the player to keep in tune, but although the frets can be a useful guide to beginners, their real purpose is to give every note the clear, ringing quality which can be heard in the open strings of the violin family.

Viols are quiet instruments, and when we listen to their music we have to concentrate. But it is worth the effort, for if they are well played they can produce a tone that is finely-drawn without being thin, and soft without being flabby. This quiet sound is partly the result of the curved bow, which is held with the palm of the hand facing upwards. The technique needed for this kind of bowing can help to lighten a dotted rhythm, so that the listener feels lifted up by it, almost as if he were dancing. And the clear tone, without any vibrato, can help the players to hear each other's entries of the tune during a Fantasia.

To Byrd and his contemporaries, the Fantasia was 'the most principal and chiefest kind of music' for strings. Byrd was particularly fond of the sort of Fantasia called 'In Nomine', which was founded on the notes of a plainsong antiphon, 'Gloria tibi Trinitas'. The slow, even notes of the chant could be given to the highest treble viol, or to the bass, or to one of the middle instruments; and there was no need for these long-drawn-out notes to be played louder than anything else, because the listeners knew that the

Ex. 6 Prelude

plainsong was the foundation of the music. Byrd wrote as many as eight *In Nomine* Fantasias, and at least one *Browning*, which was the secular equivalent, founded on a song called 'The leaves be green'. He also wrote Pavans and Galliards for viols, but most of his dances were written for virginals.

The name 'virginals' has puzzled many people. It has nothing to do with the Virgin Queen Elizabeth, although she practised the instrument every day and is said to have played it well. Musicians have suggested that the name may come from the Latin *virgula*, meaning 'a little stick', just as the word 'spinet' comes from *spina*, meaning 'a thorn'. Virginals and spinets are smaller, simpler versions of the harpsichord: each string is plucked by a quill that is attached to an upright stick. Sixteenth-century English composers always referred to the instrument as 'a pair of virginals'. They were using the word 'pair' in its old sense, not meaning 'two', but meaning 'a set', just as we sometimes refer to a step-ladder as 'a pair of steps'.

A pair of virginals was small enough to be picked up and carried from one room to another: it was the perfect instrument for music-making in the home. Byrd wrote a great many virginal pieces: some of them were Fantasias; some were Pavans and Galliards. Most of them were Variations on well-known tunes: dance tunes such as 'Sellenger's Round', and song tunes such as 'O Mistress mine', and 'Will you walk the woods so wild'. He also wrote descriptive pieces: *The Battle*, with its lively representation of trumpets and drums; and *The Bells*, which must surely have been written with the memory of those reverberating cathedral bells at Lincoln still in his mind's ear.

A page from 'My Lady Nevell's Book', 1591

Several of his pieces were published in *Parthenia*, 'the first music that ever was printed for the virginals,' but many more of them were already known in various manuscript copies. One of the most famous of these collections was 'My Lady Nevell's Book', a 1591 volume of keyboard pieces, all by Byrd, and all beautifully copied by a musician called John Baldwin, who was so excited by one of the Galliards that he wrote the words 'homo memorabilis' in the margin. Lady Nevell became Marchioness of Abergavenny, and her book is still in the possession of the family for whom it was written. It is bound in sixteenth-century leather, and Baldwin's well-proportioned diamond-shaped notes stand out boldly on each page, with every now and then a correction in fainter ink which might possibly be in Byrd's own writing.

Another famous manuscript is now known as the 'Fitzwilliam Virginal Book', because it is in the Fitzwilliam Museum at Cambridge. There are nearly two hundred and fifty pieces in it, and seventy of them are by Byrd.

The beginning of *O Mistress mine*, from Tregian's manuscript, *c.* 1609

Here the writing looks very different from Baldwin's: it is small and cramped, and it gives the impression that the copyist was having to economize in his music paper, and that he may not have had enough light to see by. The copyist was Francis Tregian, a Catholic who had been accused of plotting against the government. He was in prison for many years, and, as far as we know, he copied the virginal pieces during this time. He probably found the laborious occupation a relief and an encouragement, for, in spite of his imprisonment, he could feel that he was in close touch with those Catholic composers whose music he was writing out.

Ex. 7 *Sellenger's Round*

Ex. 8   *O Mistress mine*

Ex. 9 *Calino Casturame*

Slow and expressive

Ex. 10 *John, come kiss me now*

Very quick and energetic

Dr. John Bull: a portrait of 1589

Sir John Petre: a portrait of 1590

The title-page of *Parthenia*, 1612

Ex. 11   *Will you walk the woods so wild*

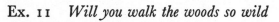

Graceful

etc.

Ex. 12   *Walsingham*

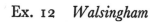

Fairly slow

quiet and smooth

etc.

Ex. 13 *Wolsey's Wild*

Fairly quick

Ex. 14 *Rowland*

Bright and majestic

VII

Music for the Catholic Church

Byrd used to go to church every Sunday in his school-days, but since the age of fifteen he had had to hear mass secretly in some private chapel, or in the ordinary living-room of a recusant's home. Most of the Catholics of his generation became members of the Church of England, for we are told that they 'did not at first discern any great fault, novelty or difference from the former religion, save only change of language'. But a minority remained true to the faith which Byrd himself believed to be 'the only hope of salvation'.

Queen Elizabeth was never a fanatical anti-Catholic. In the early days of her reign she had said: 'some think one thing, some another, and only God can say whose judgment is best'. And towards the end of her long life she could still say 'there is only one Christ Jesus and one faith: the rest is a dispute about trifles'.

At first, things were not too difficult for the English Catholics. The Queen had promised that they should be free from 'any molestation by way of inquisition of their secret opinions', and she had added: 'let it not be said that *our* reformation tendeth to cruelty'. The government, to begin with, was content with fining the recusants twelve pence a week for not going to the established church. Then the Jesuit missionaries began to arrive from the Continent. They were English Catholic refugees, many of them from Oxford or Cambridge, who had been trained to become priests in the Netherlands, in France, or in Rome. They had been sending their scholarly publications into England, pouring logical scorn on the arguments of the Protestants. (It must have been infuriating for an established bishop to be told: 'your English Church hath not yet fulfilled the age, or number of those years, which we call the years of discretion.') The Queen's advisers were dismayed. These priests were too clever. They could stand up in front of a crowd and say: 'in condemning us you condemn all your own ancestors —all the ancient priests and kings—all that was once the glory of England.'

The Tower of London in 1543, by Wyngaerde

The earliest missionaries had never meant to get mixed up with politics. They had come to encourage their fellow-Catholics, to ordain new priests, and to make converts. Before long, however, they were getting entangled with the various schemes to put Mary, Queen of Scots on the throne.

Life had been becoming more difficult for Byrd and his fellow-Catholics ever since 1570, when Pope Pius V had declared Elizabeth, 'the pretended Queen of England, to be a heretic and to have incurred the sentence of excommunication'. Many recusants were prepared to go on living quietly together, even under a heretic. But by then the arguments between Catholics and Protestants were no longer about religion: they were 'about the stability of the kingdom; about worldly prosperity'.

An Act of Parliament in 1581 had increased the fine for not going to church to £20 a month: the Jesuits indignantly described this as 'mulcting them for not repairing to their damnable schismatical service'. The Act went on to say that anyone who stayed away from church for as long as twelve months would have to pay £200, and an entry in the Public Records Office, dated February 17th, 1583, states that Byrd was one of these offenders.

Anyone 'harbouring a priest' was guilty of treason, and in the spring of 1585 a new Bill was introduced 'for the utter extirpation of Popery against Jesuits and others'. A list was drawn up of 'the places where certain recusants remove in and about the city of London'; it included Byrd's house in Harlington.

The searchers who were sent to look for the recusants used to arrive 'either in the night, or early morning', and they would 'lock the whole family up in a room by themselves and go rifling the house at their will'. On one occasion Byrd's servant arrived on horseback at a house in Buckinghamshire, and 'coming to the gate while the house was in searching, he, conceiving some [suspicion] of the company which he saw, began to ride back again apace but was overtaken and searched: there was found about him an old printed song book . . . and a letter sent from Mr Byrd of the Queen's Majesty's Chapel'.

It was in a large house on the borders of Buckinghamshire, in July 1586, that Byrd spent a week with several Catholic friends, including the Jesuit priests Henry Garnet, Robert Southwell and William Weston. Their host, who was an amateur musician, had a chapel in his house, and he had built an organ and had trained the members of his household to form a choir. Possibly it was here, in this company, that Byrd's Masses were sung for the first time. These *Three Masses*, for three, four, and five voices, were published during his life, in spite of the law that anyone singing mass should 'be committed to prison, there to remain by the space of one year'. The surviving copies of Byrd's *Masses* have no title-page, so the forbidden word may not actually have appeared in print. A seventeenth-century catalogue refers to them as *Kyries*: perhaps the publisher safeguarded himself by bringing them out under this less dangerous title.

Ex. 15 *Kyrie* from the *Mass for three voices*

The Latin motets in Byrd's 1589 *Cantiones Sacrae* keep to the permitted texts, such as psalms. But in his 1591 volume, the sacred songs contain a setting of the *Salve Regina*, an antiphon which had not been allowed to be sung since the Reformation. And in the first volume of his *Gradualia*, published in 1605, most of the motets are on forbidden subjects. By this time Byrd was no longer the holder of the licence to print music, and it is surprising that the publisher should have risked not only the threat of imprisonment for having 'caused them to be imprinted', but should also have faced the difficulty of selling works that were 'against the laws of the realm'. Many of the copies would certainly have been sold abroad, for Byrd's music was well known on the Continent. And a few of them would have been bought for the Catholic chapels in the foreign embassies in London. But some of them must have been intended for recusants to sing in their secret meeting-places, and it is unlikely that any publisher would have ventured to produce them without the powerful support of the dedicatee, Henry Howard, Earl of Northampton, who was a member of the Privy Council.

Ex. 16 Canon: *Pietas omnium virtutum*

In his Latin dedication to the 'most illustrious Henry', Byrd says that in setting these sacred words, in which the praise of God is sung, he has tried as well as he could to match their beauty with his harmonies. And he goes on to say: 'I have found in these words such a deep and hidden power that, to one who thinks upon their divine significance, the right notes, in some strange manner, come of their own accord to a wakeful and expectant mind.'

VIII

'This our Golden Age'

Byrd's contemporaries were able to speak of the time in which they were living as 'this our Golden Age'. They could boast of

> . . . *the matchless excellence*
> *Of Byrd, Bull, Dowland, Morley, and the rest*
> *Of our rare Artists (who now dim the lights*
> *Of other lands).*

And among the rest of the rare artists another forty names could be added to those four, from Alison, Attey, Bartlett and Bateson to Vautor, Weelkes, Wilbye and Youll.

This superabundance of good composers has puzzled historians. Why should there have been so much excellent music in England during the second half of the sixteenth century? Perhaps one reason is that the Elizabethan way of life encouraged the adventurous. Drake was only one among the many explorers, and twenty years after his voyage round the world the author of 'Principal Navigations and Discoveries of the English Nation' could proudly exclaim: 'What English ships did heretofore ever anchor in the mighty river of the Plate, pass and repass the impassable (in former opinion) Strait of Magellan, range along the coast of Chile, Peru, and all the backside of Nova Hispania further than any Christian ever passed, traverse the mighty breadth of the South Seas, land upon the Luzones in despite of the enemy, enter into alliance, amity, and traffic with the princes of the Moluccas and the Isle of Java, double the famous Cape of Bona Speranza, arrive at the Isle of Santa Helena, and last of all return home most richly laden with the commodities of China, as the subjects of this now flourishing monarchy have done?'

They seem a race apart, these quick-witted Englishmen who explored everything they came across. 'I have taken all knowledge to be my province' announced Bacon, and he faced the task of learning all that could be learnt as if he were setting out on the liveliest of adventures.

Liveliness was something that Elizabethans demanded from all their artists. In their tapestries and paintings they were not content with figures that looked as if they were 'standing upon a cloth or board': they wanted them to look 'as if they were acting upon a stage'. Actors were taught 'to move in music' and were told to 'see the words agree to the gesture as the dance doth to the sound of the instrument'. When Hamlet warns the Players not to 'mouth' their speeches or to 'saw the air too much' with their hands he is reminding them that even in the 'whirlwind of passion' their acting should have the smoothness of a superb technique to achieve true liveliness.

Shakespeare was one among the many Golden Age dramatists who were also poets. They chose words that were 'sinewy and strong', aiming at 'clearness of representation' in their 'high and hearty invention'. In setting their verses to music, Byrd and the other Elizabethan composers were able to 'couple the words and notes lovingly together', for the poets themselves had skilfully succeeded in making the sound of each line agree with its sense.

Unfortunately, the sense of Elizabethan English is not always clear to twentieth-century readers. There are several reasons for this. To begin with, there are the many words that have now changed their original meaning, such as our 'presently', which was their *immediately*, *let* ('hinder'), *prevent* ('anticipate') and *artificial* ('displaying art or skill'). There are also the differences in punctuation, which often make an Elizabethan sentence seem as unnecessarily complicated as some of the Epistles of St. Paul. There are the frequent puns, which seem tiresome to a modern reader, but which Shakespeare was very fond of. (His allusions to 'burdens' and 'frets', or to 'counter' for counter-tenor, 'mean' for middle voice, and 'base' for bass, show that his audiences must have been familiar with a good many of the terms used in music.) Then there are the 'correspondences'. The Elizabethans believed that everything in creation had its own 'sovereign' of acknowledged excellence. 'The lion,' they said, 'is king of beasts, the eagle chief of birds. The whale among fishes; Jupiter's oak the forest's king. Among flowers we most admire the rose; among stones we value above all the diamond; metals, gold and silver.' This sovereignty explains why sixteenth-century plays and poems so often refer to the king as a lion and the queen as a rose. To the Elizabethans there was nothing in the least quaint about these parallels or correspondences. They had been taught that God had 'set degrees in all his glorious works', with 'man over man, beast over beast, bird over bird, and fish over fish'. They knew what Shakespeare was talking about when he said:

> *Take but degree away, untune that string,*
> *And hark, what discord follows.*

One of the greatest authorities on the Elizabethan age, Dr. E. M. W. Tillyard, has said that the delight which their poets took in finding correspondences everywhere was part of the medieval tradition of striving after unity. In his book, *The Elizabethan World Picture*, he says: 'The amount of intellectual and emotional satisfaction these correspondences afforded is difficult both to imagine and to overestimate. What to us is merely silly might for an Elizabethan be a solemn or joyful piece of evidence that he lived in an ordered universe.'

The Elizabethan composers were not theorists: they were practical musicians. But they knew about the need for order in their own art. Beauty, to them, was 'Comeliness, the child of Order', a fair disposing 'of things and actions in fit time and place'. One of Byrd's great contemporaries, Orlando Gibbons, said: 'it is proportion that beautifies everything; this whole Universe consists of it, and music is measured by it.' There was no need for them to question the mathematical proportions on which their rhythms and harmonies were founded. It was their good fortune to be able to keep what they needed of their medieval traditions while welcoming the newest inventions and discoveries. In their houses they continued to strew rushes on the floor, in spite of the spectacular decorations on their walls and the elaborate patterns on their ceilings. And in their music they could write an *In Nomine* on a solemn medieval chant while feeling free to combine its slow notes with their latest devices in agile cross-rhythms. They were true explorers, but they were not tempted to try and revolutionize the music of their time.

Byrd and the other 'rare artists' were never troubled by any thoughts of writing for posterity: they were far too busy writing pavans and madrigals and fantasias for the amateur dancers and singers and players who were actually asking for their music. Nor were they troubled by trying to please the critics: in fact, they said what they thought about their music critics with a freedom that has not yet been equalled in the twentieth century; protesting against 'those who from their ignorance, lack of artistic taste, or warped natures are unable to judge fairly', and against those 'petty people who examine every work minutely, solely to pick as many flaws as possible'. The composer Thomas Ford pitched upon one unfortunate critic for a particularly violent attack in his printed introduction to a volume of songs: 'thou never thinkst well of any, and wert in thyself so unskilful as thy tutor from the first hour could never make thee sing in tune. Thou art a lump of deformity without fashion, bred in the bowels of disdain.'

Did these Golden Age composers know what they were achieving in their own works? Probably not. But they were aware of the power of music. Robert Jones, in his 1608 volume of songs, says:

> Almost all our knowledge is drawn through the senses: they are the soul's intelligencers whereby she passeth into the world and the world into her: and amongst all of them, there is none so learned as the ear, none hath obtained so excellent an art, so delicate, so abstruse, so spiritual, that it catcheth up wild sounds in the air and brings them under a government not to be expressed but done, and done by no skill but its own.

This is the authentic voice of the practical composer, insisting that music must speak for itself. It is a reminder that the golden age was not legendary, but real: in the language of the 'correspondences' it was the greatest age for music that England has yet known. And Byrd was the greatest among the many composers, being acknowledged by his contemporaries as the 'Phoenix' or paragon of his time.

IX

The Last Years at Stondon Massey

Byrd spent the last thirty years of his life in the Essex village of Stondon Massey. It was in 1593, the year when there was a terrible plague in London, that he left Harlington and brought his family to live in a house called Stondon Place. He could not afford to buy it, but he rented it on a long lease and made it more comfortable to live in, 'erecting chimneys and bringing water into the house in pipes of lead'. The property included Malperdus Farm, which was down a narrow, winding lane between Malperdus woods and 'the Parson's Bushes', a plot of land known as 'the glebe' because it was used by clergymen of the parish. Before long he was having difficulties with his tenant at Malperdus, who refused to pay his rent. The tenant, whose name was Dionysius Lolly, was a churchwarden of the parish and an enemy of all recusants. He accused Byrd of taking from him 'certain rooms' at Malperdus and of making him do some 'hedging and ditching' which had not been mentioned in the lease. Byrd took the case to court in 1595, asking that justice might be done, and in the end Dionysius Lolly was defeated.

Soon after this there was another lawsuit over a right of way between Stondon and the village of Kelvedon Hatch. Parson Nobbs, rector of Stondon, 'caused William Byrd to be indicted for stopping up a common highway through Malperdus wood'. The lane had not been used since 1550. Parson Nobbs wanted it re-opened, as it joined his glebe lands. Byrd was determined to keep it closed, so that he and his family could walk through the woods without being seen when they went to hear mass in the house of his Catholic friend, John Wright, who lived at Kelvedon Hall. The lawsuit dragged on for years. Witnesses were called, and old men spoke of the ancient highway 'from the uttermost of their remembrance'. Eventually the case was decided in Byrd's favour, and ever since then the lane has come to an end at Malperdus Farm, and there is still no right of way through those woods to Kelvedon Hatch.

An entry in the Stondon records for 1595 states that 'Mr Wm. Byrd and his wife, and his son and his wife and his two daughters have not come to our church since they came into our parish to dwell.' The family was in perpetual trouble because of the law against recusants. Every year they had to appear at the Archdeacon's Court at Romford, and twice a year they had to go to Chelmsford for the Quarter Sessions, and there were proceedings against them at the Assizes. Year after year they paid heavy fines. The churchwardens at Stondon complained that Byrd had been influencing young John Wright, 'son and heir of John Wright of Kelvedon', and that Byrd's wife had 'appointed business on the Sabbath Day for her servants of purpose to keep them from church'.

In all these Essex accounts of their recusancy Byrd's wife's name is given as 'Ellen'. So little is known about his personal life that historians are not able to say whether this was a second wife, or whether the name was a mis-spelling for the Juliana who was mentioned in the Harlington records until the mid-fifteen-eighties. No family letters have survived.

We know more about some of his friends than about his wife and children. There are detailed descriptions of the early life of his near neighbour Sir John Petre, because the household account books at his home in Ingatestone were carefully kept; we are told exactly how much was paid for new strings for the lute or for repairing the virginals. Sir John was an excellent amateur musician, and he liked to invite singers and players to make music in the long gallery at Ingatestone Hall; during the Christmas holiday of 1589–90, before Byrd had left Harlington, Petre sent a servant 'to fetch Mr Byrd down from London' with five other musicians. He showed great sympathy with recusants, and the fact that Ingatestone was only five miles from Stondon Massey was probably the chief reason for the family's decision to move into Essex.

Byrd now had less work to do in London. The Queen was growing old. Until the very last year of her life she still enjoyed watching country dancing in the Privy Chamber, following the cadence 'with her head, hand and foot', and being 'exceedingly pleased' with the energetic Irish tunes; 'but', as Lord Worcester said to one of his friends, 'in winter, *Lullaby*, an old song of Mr Byrd's, will be more in request, I think.'

When she died in 1603, Byrd went to London for her funeral, and walked in procession at the head of the singing-men of the Chapel Royal, immediately behind Dr. John Bull, the organist, and Nathaniel Giles, the Master of the Children.

The Gentlemen of the Chapel Royal were grateful to the new king,

Lord Howard of Effingham, by Daniel Mytens

Above, a boy singer and viol players, from a contemporary picture of the life of Sir Henry Unton; *below*, Ingatestone Hall in Essex

A page from Sir John Petre's part-book, *c.* 1580

James I, because at the very beginning of his reign he increased their salaries by £10 a year. They recorded 'his kingly bounty', wishing him 'blessings both spiritual and temporal'.

The Catholics were also grateful to King James at that time, for it seemed that he might be able to help their cause. At the opening of his first Parliament he had said: 'I acknowledge the Roman Church to be our Mother Church, although defiled with some infirmities. My mind was ever free from persecution of my subjects in matters of conscience, as I hope that those of that profession within this kingdom have a proof since my coming.' But the Gunpowder Plot put an end to the recusants' hopes for the future. Several of Byrd's friends were involved. The ninth Earl of Northumberland, the son of his former patron, was imprisoned for fifteen years and fined £11,000, although he was innocent. The Jesuit priest, Henry Garnet, was hanged as a traitor, because one of his penitents had told him of the plot and he had said nothing about it, believing that 'what sin soever is heard in confession, it cannot lawfully be revealed'. Many of Byrd's Catholic friends

Ex. 18 *Deo gratias*

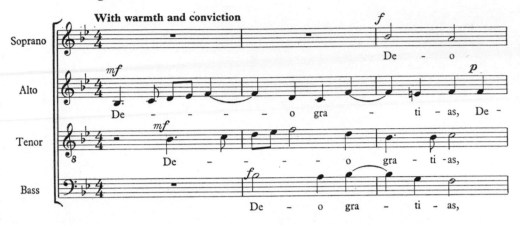

in Essex signed the recusants' statement to the authorities, saying: 'concerning the late conspiracies, we were neither consenting, approving or applauding, but utterly condemning them as barbarous, both to God and man.' They knew they were in danger.

Byrd owed his safety to the help of his influential friends, and he was particularly grateful to John Petre, now Baron Petre of Writtle. Without such a patron, it is unlikely that he would have been able to publish his second book of *Gradualia* in 1607. In his Latin dedication to Petre he said:

> Since, relying on divine mercy, I have reached such a span of years that I have seen many of my pupils in the realm of music—men most excellently equipped in that art—pass from life while I survive; and since in my own life I consider that the richness of divine bounty has been conferred and indeed showered upon me; my mind is afire, remembering my faith, my duty, and my devotion to God, to leave behind me for future generations, in however small a measure, some public testimony of a heart that is grateful. And so, at this advanced age, I have tried, however unworthy and inadequate I may be, to put notes, as a crown, to certain holy praises in the Christian service. And, since from your household— which is most friendly to me and mine—these travails in music have for the most part sprung, and have from that kindly warmth brought forth richer fruit; so accept, most generous lord, these little flowers, gathered, almost, from your own garden and due to be given to you as tithe; and let it not be a burden to you to guard these last works of mine, so that they may go forth into the world to the glory of the most glorious and mighty God, to the magnifying of your own renown, and to the delight of all who worship the muses.

The next few years were not as peaceful as they should have been, for Byrd was involved in another tiresome lawsuit. This time it was with a Mrs. Shelley, the widow of a former owner of Stondon Place. She wanted to live there herself, and she tried to turn him out of the house. She lost her case, but a few years later she wrote a long letter to Lord Salisbury, complaining that Byrd had disgraced her with her 'honourable friends and others of great quality, persuading them that she was a woman of no good conscience'; that he had used 'vile and bitter words'; and that when he was told that he had no right to Stondon Place 'he said that if he could not hold it by right he would hold it by might'. Lord Salisbury realized that this could not be true of the man who was 'never without reverence to be named of the musicians', and he saw that Mrs. Shelley was lying because she pre-

tended to be poor when she was really quite rich. He refused to have anything to do with her 'grievances', and handed her petition to the court,
saying: 'Let her represent [it] unto the Barons, who will take some leisure
to hear her complaint, for I have none.' Mrs. Shelley died in 1610, and,
with the help of Lord Petre, Byrd was able to buy Stondon Place. Now, at
last, he could look forward to remaining there quietly for the rest of his life.

He had spoken of the motets in *Gradualia II* as his 'last works', but in 1611
he published another book of *Psalms, Songs and Sonnets*, 'some solemn, others
joyful; framed to the life of the words'. In his introduction he said:

> The natural inclination and love to the art of music, wherein I have spent
> the better part of mine age, have been so powerful in me, that even in my
> old years which are desirous of rest, I cannot contain myself from taking
> some pains therein. These are like to be my last travails in this kind.

His last duty as a member of the Chapel Royal was to attend the funeral
of Queen Anne in 1619. Visits to London must have been very exhausting
for him, but his patron Lord Worcester allowed him to stay in his house: it
was one of the magnificent houses in the Strand, with gardens leading down
to the River Thames.

In the winter of 1622 he made his will, in which he mentioned his wishes
for his funeral:

> My body to be honestly buried in that parish and place where it shall
> please God to take me out of this life, which I humbly desire, if so it shall
> please God, may be in the parish of Stondon where my dwelling is. And
> then to be buried near unto the place where my wife lies buried, or else
> whereas God and the time shall permit and suffer.

He died at Stondon on July 4th, 1623. He was buried, as far as we know,
in Stondon churchyard, but there is no tombstone to mark the position of
the grave. Recusants were allowed by law to be buried side by side with
their Protestant fellow-Christians, but it is unlikely that the churchwardens
would have allowed even a famous Catholic to have an inscription over his
head. Byrd, however, needed no written epitaph, since he had already won
'such a name as will never perish so long as music endures'.

X

Byrd's Music Today

Three hundred years after Byrd's death, a tablet in his memory was placed in Stondon Massey church. We are told that 'even in musical circles the question was being asked, "Who *was* Byrd?"' Most people knew *Non nobis*, and several of his English anthems were still sung regularly in cathedrals. But the Latin motets were practically unknown at the beginning of this century, and only a few enthusiasts were interested in the virginal pieces.

Elizabethan madrigals were no longer in fashion by the end of the seventeenth century, and very few of them had survived to be sung in those eighteenth-century informal open-air concerts which were held in the London parks known as 'Pleasure Gardens', or in nineteenth-century choral societies. Then, in the last years of the nineteenth century, there was a revival of interest in Elizabethan poetry, and the words from the song-books were published in anthologies. People began asking about the music, but when they tried to sing the few madrigals that were available in print, they took everything much too slowly, because the notes nearly always seemed to be minims and semibreves. (See page 70.)

This slow and stately style of singing made nonsense of the cheerful songs with the 'fa la la' choruses, and it worried a young canon of Windsor called Edmund Horace Fellowes. He began to think about the possibility of bringing out some madrigals in a modern notation that would look easier to sing. It happened that one summer afternoon in 1911, when he was on holiday in Devonshire, the young lady who was his tennis partner asked him how it was that although there were complete editions of the works of the poets of Shakespeare's day, there were no such editions of any of the works of the madrigal composers. The question was like a challenge, and Fellowes decided to begin the very next week on the colossal task of editing the music of the sixteenth-century English composers. The volumes were published year by year, and were welcomed by enthusiastic musicians who could

The treble part of 'See those sweet eyes', from *Songs of Sundry Natures*, 1589

hardly wait until the next one appeared.

Fellowes wrote a book about Byrd, having searched for every scrap of information that was to be found. He also embarked on an edition of all the vocal music Byrd had written. Many of the original copies had been lost, or had only survived in arrangements for lute solo. Sixteenth-century composers did not keep their manuscripts, and the only authentic copies of Byrd's vocal music are the printed part-books which he himself corrected. ('If there be any dissonance,' he told his singers in 1588, 'blame not the Printer, who—I do assure thee—through his great pains and diligence doth here deliver to thee a perfect and true copy.')

While Fellowes was editing the music he often had to work from incomplete sets of part-books, which meant that he had to re-construct the missing voice-parts himself. (I remember seeing him in the British Museum library

70

during the nineteen-twenties: the look of concentration on his face was almost frightening.) Other editors have brought out more recent publications of sixteenth-century music: they all owe Fellowes a tremendous debt of gratitude.

The search for the missing copies still goes on. A few days before this chapter was begun, the news arrived that an unknown Byrd *Litany* had been discovered: it was in a manuscript that had been owned by the same family for three hundred and fifty years. And there is still a need for new editions, not only because the Elizabethan composers left so much to the intelligence of their performers, but also because their system of notation was so very different from ours. They had no bar-lines in their songs, and they did not share our preference for writing each word directly underneath the note that belongs to it. They never used any tempo indications such as 'Allegro', although their longest notes were often meant to be sung or played very quickly. They had no written signs for 'loud' or 'soft'. Instead of having time-signatures, they referred to 'the Perfect of the More', or 'the Imperfect of the Less'. Instead of keeping to our rules for accidentals, they often left it to the performer to guess whether a note should be sharp or flat. (For instance, in *Wolsey's Wild* on page 51, the quaver B at the end of the last bar but one has no written flat in the Fitzwilliam Virginal Book: it could be either a flat or a natural.) 'Let your ear be judge' was the advice that Byrd's pupil, Morley, gave in his book for beginners.

Editing Byrd's music needs courage. But it is worth taking the plunge, because today there are more and more people wanting to sing and play what he has written. His works are strong and satisfying, and everything sounds and feels in the right place at the right time. For he is still 'the most assured friend to all that love or learn music'.

Suggestions for Further Reading

William Byrd, E. H. Fellowes (Oxford)
The Pelican History of Music, Vol. 2, ed., A. Robertson & D. Stevens
Musical Instruments through the Ages, ed., A. Baines (Pelican)
Tudor England, S. T. Bindoff (Pelican)
Illustrated English Social History, Vol. 2, G. M. Trevelyan (Pelican)
Life in Shakespeare's England, J. D. Wilson (Pelican)
Elizabethan & Jacobean Prose, ed., K. Muir (Pelican)
The Centuries' Poetry, Vol. I, ed., D. K. Roberts (Pelican)
The Elizabethan World Picture, E. M. Tillyard (Peregrine)
Life in Elizabethan England, A. H. Dodd (Batsford)
How they lived (1485–1700), M. Harrison & O. M. Royston (Blackwell)
Tudor Food and Pastimes, F. G. Emmison (Benn)
    Three 'Jackdaws' (Cape):
Henry VIII and the dissolution of the Monasteries
Elizabeth I
The Gunpowder Plot

Short Summary of Byrd's Works

Latin Church Music

Cantiones sacrae (with Tallis, 1575)
Cantiones sacrae I (1589)
Cantiones sacrae II (1591)
Three Masses (*c.* 1605)
Gradualia I (1605)
Gradualia II (1607)
    (and at least 40 other motets)

English Church Music (dates not known)

First 'Short' Service
Second Service
Third Service
The 'Great' Service
    (and at least 30 anthems and psalms in addition to those in the following publications)

Madrigals, etc.

Psalms, Sonnets, and Songs of Sadness and Piety (1588)
Songs of Sundry Natures (1589)
Psalms, Songs and Sonnets (1611)
    (and at least 12 other madrigals)

Songs with Strings

16 sacred songs
30 secular songs
    (in many of these the string parts are incomplete: see Chapter X)

Music for Strings

14 Fantasias
8 'In Nomine' Fantasias
1 Browning
Pavan and Galliard

Music for Keyboard

More than a hundred pieces, mostly for virginals, including Fantasias, dances, and variations on song tunes. Also Preludes, Voluntaries, Variations on the Hexachord, and Fantasias on plainsong melodies which were probably intended for organ.

Index

Alison, Richard (late 16th century), English composer, 59

Anne of Denmark (1574–1619), wife of James I, 68

Antiphon, 16, 42, 56

Appleby, Thomas (died c. 1562), English composer and organist, 22

Ariosto, Ludovico (1474–1533), Italian poet, 37

Attey, John (died c. 1640), English composer and lutenist, 59

Bacon, Francis; Baron Verulam, Viscount St. Albans (1561–1626), English statesman and author, 60

Baldwin, John (died 1615), English musician, 45

Bartlett, John (late 16th century), English composer and lutenist, 59

Battle, The, 43

Bateson, Thomas (c. 1570–1630), English composer and organist, 59

Bells, The, 43

Birley, Juliana, *see* Byrd, Juliana

Book of Common Prayer, The, 22

British Museum, The, 18, 70

Browning, 43

Bull, Dr. John (1563–1628), English composer and organist, 59, 64

Byrd, Christopher (1569–c. 1614), Byrd's eldest son, 24

Byrd, 'Ellen', possibly Byrd's second wife, 64, 68

Byrd, Juliana (*née* Birley), Byrd's wife, 24, 27, 64

Byrd, Thomas (early 16th century), possibly Byrd's father, 17

Campion, Edmund (1540–81), Jesuit, 40

Canon, 16, 19, 33

Cantiones Sacrae (1575), 28–9

Cantiones Sacrae (1589), 56

Cantiones Sacrae (1591), 56

Chapel Royal, The, 17, 24, 25, 27–8, 30, 55, 64–5, 68

'Correspondences', 60–1, 62

Cranmer, Thomas (1489–1556), Archbishop of Canterbury, 22, 23

Day, John (1522–84), English printer, 23

Dowland, John (1563–1626), English composer and lutenist, 59

Drake, Sir Francis (c. 1540–96), English seaman, 59

Edward VI (1537–53), 22, 23

Elizabeth I (1533–1603), 22, 23, 25, 27, 28–9, 30–1, 43, 53, 54–5, 64

Elizabethan World Picture, The, 61

Fantasia, 16, 42–3

Fellowes, Canon Edmund Horace (1870–1951), English musical editor, 69–71

Fitzwilliam Virginal Book, The, 44–5, 71

Ford, Thomas (c. 1580–1648), English composer and lutenist, 61–2

Index

Galliard, 16, 43, 44

Garnet, Henry (1555–1606), Jesuit, 55, 65

Gibbons, Orlando (1583–1625), English composer and organist, 61

Giles, Nathaniel (c. 1558–1633), English composer and organist, 64

'Gloria tibi Trinatis', 42

Gradualia I (1605), 56

Gradualia II (1607), 67, 68

Greenwich Palace, 25, 30

Gunpowder Plot, The, 65–7

Hamlet, 60

Hampton Court, 25

Harlington, 27, 55, 63, 64

Harpsichord, 43

Hatton, Sir Christopher (1540–91), Lord Chancellor, 31

Henry VIII (1491–1547), 17, 18, 22, 25

Hexachord, 23

Hunsdon, Lord (1524–96), Lord Chamberlain, 40

Imitation (polyphonic), 33

Ingatestone Hall, 64

In Nomine, 42, 43, 61

James I (1566–1625), 17, 64–5

Jesuit missionaries, 53–5

Jones, Robert (died c. 1617), English composer and lutenist, 62

Kelvedon Hatch, 63–4

King's College Chapel, Cambridge, 18

Kyries, 55

La Virginella, 37, 40

'Leaves be green, The', 43

Lincoln Cathedral, 19, 21–2, 23–4, 30, 43

Litany, 71

Lullaby, 64

Madrigal, 16, 37, 69

Malperdus, 63

Mary, Queen of Scots (1542–87), 54

Mary Tudor (1516–58), 17, 22, 30

Masses, Three, 55

Monasteries, 18

Monte, Phillippe de (c. 1521–1603), Flemish composer, 17

Morley, Thomas (1557–1603), English composer, 31–3, 36, 59, 71

Motet, 16, 18, 19, 23, 27–8, 56, 68, 69

Musica Transalpina, 37

'My Lady Nevell's Book', 44

Nonesuch Palace, 25

Non nobis, Domine, 19, 69

Northampton; Henry Howard, Earl of (1540–1614), 56, 58

Northumberland, 8th Earl of (1532–85), 31, 65

'O Mistress mine', 43

Part-books, 25, 37, 70

Parthenia, 44

Pavan (or Pavane), 16, 43

Petre, Sir John; 1st Baron Petre of Writtle (1549–1613), 64, 67, 68

Philip II of Spain (1527–98), 17

Pius V, Pope (1504–72), 54

Plain and Easy Introduction to Practical Music, A, 31–3, 36

Plainchant, *see* Plainsong

Plainsong, 16, 19, 22, 42–3

Polyphonic music, 16, 18, 23, 33

Power, Leonel (15th century), English composer, 19

Psalms, Songs and Sonnets, 1611, 68

Psalms, Sonnets and Songs, 1588, 37, 40

Reasons briefly set down to persuade everyone to learn to sing, 36, 37

Recusants (from the Latin *recusare*: to reject a cause), 27, 31, 40, 53–5, 56, 64, 65–7, 68

Richmond Palace, 25

Ridley, Nicholas (c. 1500–55), Bishop of London, 22

78

Index

Round, 16, 19

St. George's Chapel, Windsor, 18, 25
Salisbury; Robert Cecil, 1st Earl of (*c.* 1563–1612), 67–8
Salve Regina, 56
'Sellenger's Round', 43
Shakespeare, William (1564–1616), 60, 61, 69
Songs of Sundry Natures, 40, 41
Southwell, Robert (*c.* 1561–95), Jesuit, 55
Spem in alium, 18
Spinet, 43
Stondon Massey, 63–4, 67–8, 69
Syon House, 25

Tallis, Thomas (*c.* 1505–85), English composer and organist, 18, 19, 23, 24, 25, 28–9, 30–1
Tancred and Gismunda, 31
Tillyard, Dr. E. M. W. (1889–1962), English writer and lecturer, 61
Tregian, Francis (*c.* 1574–1619), English musician, 45

Variations, 23, 43
Vautor, Thomas (late 16th century), English composer, 59
Viols, 41, 42–3
Virginals, 43–5, 69

Waltham Abbey, 18
Weelkes, Thomas (*c.* 1575–1623), English composer, 59
Weston, William (1550–1615), Jesuit, 55
Whitehall Palace, 25
Wilbye, John (1574–1638), English composer, 59
'Will you walk the woods so wild', 43
Wolsey's Wild, 71
Worcester; Edward, 4th Earl of (1553–1628), Lord Privy Seal, 64, 68

Yonge, Nicholas (died 1619), English musician, 37
Youll, Henry (late 16th century), English composer, 59